Are Church Age Saints in the Olivet Discourse?

A Biblical Explanation of Matthew 24-25
The Pre-Tribulational View Verified

By Cooper P Abrams III, Ph.D.

August, 2019

All Rights Reserved

Copyright August 2019 by Cooper P. Abrams, III

Are Church Age Saints in the Olivet Discourse?
A Biblical Explanation of Matthew 24-25
The Pre-Tribulational View Verified

Printed in the United States of America. The author of this work has quoted writers of articles and books. This does not mean that the author endorses or recommends the works of others. If the author quotes someone, it does not mean he agrees with all the author's tenets, statements, concepts, or words, whether in the work quoted or any other work.

ISBN 978-1-7339247-8-8

All Scripture taken from the King James Bible.

All rights reserved solely by the author. No part of this work may be reproduced without the expressed consent of the author, except for brief quotes, whether by electronic, photocopying, recording, or information storage and retrieval systems.

Address All Inquiries to:
Cooper P. Abrams, III
Bible Truth Web Site
http://bible-truth.org
435 452-1716
cpabrams3@gmail.com

Published by:
The Old Paths Publications
142 Gold flume Way,
Cleveland, GA
TOP@theoldpathspublications.com
www.theoldpathspublications.com
All rights reserved.

DEDICATION

This book, with all my years of ministry and study, is dedicated to my Savior, the Lord Jesus Christ who forgave all my sins and has given me eternal life. Paul stated regarding his ministry, "And I thank Christ Jesus our Lord, who hath enabled me, for that he counted me faithful, putting me into the ministry; (1 Timothy 1:12) Note Paul did not say he was worthy of being used of the Lord, but rather counted faithful. Although I have failed many times during all these many years, my desire and determination has always been to be faithful and never to compromise God's Word.

I realized the truth that John 1:1 states, "In the beginning was the Word, and the Word was with God, and the Word was God." (John 1:1) Jesus is the literal very Word of God and to compromise, distort, and not be faithful in my studies, preaching and teaching of the Word, would be degrading the very Person of my Savior Jesus Christ, because He and His Word are synonymous.

Further, I am grateful to the many teachers I have had over these many years who taught me both in person and their writings.

TABLE OF CONTENTS

DEDICATION iii
TABLE OF CONTENTS iv
Are Church Age Saints in the Olivet Discourse? 1
   A Biblical Explanation of Matthew 24:1 - 25:46 1
   False Views Espoused from a False Interpretation 4
   The Purpose of this Paper 6
   The Two Questions Answered by Christ Matthew 24-25 ... 9
   Christians in this Age are the Body and Bride of Christ ... 12
   The Events of the Seven Year Tribulation are the 16
   End of the Old Testament Dispensation 16
   Israel Will Be Restored by God 24
   God Will Give Israel Their Promised Kingdom 29
   Jesus Preparing Disciples for His Return to Heaven 36
   The Kingdom of Heaven Presented & Temporarily Withdrawn 39
   Comparing the Good News for Israel and to Christians in This Age 41
   The Book of Acts Reveals the Transition from the Kingdom Offered to Israel to the Present Church Age 44
   Christians In the Church Age Will Not Go into or Through Any Part of The Seven Year Tribulation. (Rev. 3:10) 51
   The Imminent Return of Christ. 57
   God Sends Strong Delusion to Unbelievers 64
   Who Reject Christ In the Church Age 64
   The Last Days 66
   Daniel's 70th Week 70
   The Great Tribulation Begins. 70
   Matthew 24-25 70
   The Sequence of These Events 73
   Matthew 24 73
   The Second Coming of Christ 78
   The Rapture of the Lost 81
   The Marriage Supper of The Lamb 83
   Matthew 25 83
   The Second Coming of Christ 87
   The Judgment of Nations 88

THE OLIVET DISCOURSE

Conclusion 97
ABOUT THE AUTHOR 101

Are Church Age Saints in the Olivet Discourse?

A Biblical Explanation of Matthew 24:1 - 25:46

By Cooper P Abrams III, Ph.D.
All rights reserved.

The Olivet Discourse of Matthew 24-25, without a question, is one of the most misunderstood and subsequently one of the most misinterpreted passages in the New Testament. Often overlooked is the subject of the discourse in which Jesus was answering the questions of His disciples about the end of the age. The discord has come from not understanding what age the Lord was describing which is the context of His statements. The result has brought forth various eschatological views such as the Pre-Wrath, Mid, and Post Tribulational and a host of other contradictory theories that have caused great confusion among today's Christians. Paul plainly states, "For God is not *the author* of confusion, but of peace, as in all churches of the saints." (1 Corinthians 14:33) Therefore, the problem is not that God has not made the passages clear, but that man has applied a faulty interpretation.

The heart of the problem is that many interpreters have not applied sound rules of hermeneutics and have made the serious mistake of mixing God's plans and purpose for Israel with that of the Christians in this the Church Age.

This book is a verse by verse, careful exegetical examination of the Olivet Discourse that shows that Church Age saints are not present during the Tribulation. Further, it demonstrates that the New Testament teaches the Pre-Tribulational rapture of Christians in this dispensation.

All believers of all ages are saved the same way by faith in the Jesus Christ. The Old Testament saints were looking forward to His redemptive work in the future as God had promised. Church Age believers are looking back to the coming and finished work of Jesus Christ in suffering and dying for the sins of the world. Yet, God makes a distinction between how He works with Israel and also Christians in this age. God has a different plan and purpose for Christians in this age that is distinct from the Old Testament. God is not finished with His chosen people and the Old Testament dispensation. If this truth is ignored and not applied in the interpretation of Matthew 24-25 the results will produce a misconception of the events of the end times.

The Lord's Olivet discourse deals with the end of the Old Testament age or dispensation in which Jesus lived. All four Gospels record events that occurred in the Old Testament period. That dispensation isn't completed, but was put on hold temporarily until the time of the Gentiles is finished. (Luke 21:24) This is a vital truth that must be considered in interpreting the Lord's message on the Mount of Olives.   God will once again start His prophetic clock and finish the 490 years of Daniel's prophecy in the coming 70th Week that is the coming seven-year Tribulation.

It is a common mistake in interpreting Matthew 24-25 to conclude that this passage is written to describe the end time events of the present church age. Instead, these events are actually a description of the coming seven-year Tribulation. It is a mistake to interpret them as being a part of the current Church Age.

False Views Espoused from a False Interpretation

For example, because of the similarities of Matthew 24:40-41 with the rapture of 1 Thessalonians 4:13-18, some have concluded that this is the rapture of believers in the Church Age and places it within the Tribulation. They then preclude that Christians will be on earth and will be present through part of the Tribulation. This interpretation causes them to establish the rapture in the chronology of the seven years. The offshoot of this has been a Pre-Wrath, Mid, Post Tribulation rapture. Ignoring the sound biblical principles of interpretation causes great confusion concerning Christ's coming for Christians at the rapture, and with His Second coming at the end of the Tribulation. The details of the rapture and the Second Coming at the end of the Tribulation are clearly different.

Other related views espoused are the Post and Amillennialism based on their false understanding of Matthew 25:31-46. Both of these views teach there will not be a literal 1000-year reign of Christ in the Kingdom as Revelation 20:4-6 describes. Further, they discount God's promises of the Kingdom to Israel. They assume this passage to be describing a single end time judgment with the saved or sheep on one side and the lost or goats on the other side referred to as the "Sheep and Goat Judgment." This interpretation does not take into account the BEMA judgment of 1 Corinthian 3:10-15 for Church Age saints and the final judgment of the unsaved at the Great White Throne Judgment of Revelation 20:11-15. The result of these false views has caused a shadow over the Lord's discourse and biblical eschatology.

The Purpose of this Paper

The following is presented as a response to explain hermeneutically that these are incorrect views and Matthew 24-25 supports the Pre-Tribulation rapture and Pre-Millennial view of eschatology. A correct interpretation will show that the Church Age saints are not in view in the Christ's Olivet Discourse.

The context of the Olivet Discourse is established by Matthew 24:3. It is critical in interpreting a passage of God's word to fully understand the context in which Jesus' statements are made. The context establishes who Jesus was addressing, when the address is made; the subject of His discourse; and the historical and cultural situation at that time.

Critical to understanding Matthew 24-25 is realizing the disciples knew nothing of this present Church Age and their questions were addressing the end times as related to Israel. Jesus in Matthew 16:18-19 had prophesied of the establishment of His *ekklesia,* but did not give them further details until after His resurrection as Acts 1:1-8 records. (This will be addressed later)

Clearly, on the minds of His disciples was the end of their present period of the Old Testament when the Messiah would restore the Kingdom to Israel. This was why the disciples asked their questions. To understand this, one must take into consideration the preceding events the disciples had witnessed.

They had seen Jesus weeping over Jerusalem as Luke 19:41-44 recorded in which He predicted the 70 A.D. destruction of the city. They witnessed His purging of the Temple of the money changers. They repeatedly had heard His teaching and parables and had witnessed the violent response of the chief priests and scribes. Jesus had spoken of the alarming details of the destruction of the Temple and coming events.

Luke then records a shorter but parallel account of the Olivet Discourse. Luke 21:5-7 states the context of the disciple's questions. "And as some spake of the temple, how it was adorned with goodly stones and gifts, he said, As for these things which ye behold, the days will come, in the which there shall not be left one stone upon another, that shall not be thrown down. And they asked him, saying, Master, but when shall these things be? and what sign will there be when these things shall come to pass?" (Luke 21:5-7)

THE OLIVET DISCOURSE

Jesus had consistently presented Himself to be the promised Messiah and the disciples were aware that He said he was the Messiah. They heard Him affirm He was the Messias to the Samaritan woman. "The woman saith unto him, I know that Messiahs cometh, which is called Christ: when he is come, he will tell us all things. Jesus saith unto her, I that speak unto thee am he." (John 4:25-26)

Mark records that Jesus attested to this at his trial before the high priest, "But he held his peace, and answered nothing. Again the high priest asked him, and said unto him, Art thou the Christ, the Son of the Blessed? And Jesus said, I am: and ye shall see the Son of man sitting on the right hand of power, and coming in the clouds of heaven." (Mark 14:61-62)

The Two Questions Answered by the Lord in Matthew 24-25

The disciples asked the Lord the two specific questions, ". . . what shall these things be? and what shall be the sign of thy coming, and the end of the world." The word, "coming" is *parousia*, and basically means, "presence" or "arrival." (See 1 Cor. 16:17, 2 Cor. 7:7) The "*parousia*" refers to the Second Coming of the Lord Jesus, the Messiah, at the end of the age. Jesus will come and purge the earth of sinners and then fifty days later begins the Millennium which is the promised Kingdom to Israel.

The word translated "*world*" is the word *aion*, and means "age or a period of time." The question the disciples asked was, "Tell us, when shall these things be? and what shall be the sign of thy coming, and of the end of the world *(this present period)?*" The age when Christ preached the Olivet Discourse was the period just prior to His crucifixion, which was the Old Testament dispensation. This is the period Jesus was explaining. The present dispensation of the Church Age had not begun. The "age" refers to Israel's history and the end of the Old Testament dispensation. This is not referring to the coming rapture of the Church Age

THE OLIVET DISCOURSE

saints in this the "*ekklesia aion*" (Church Age) which He instituted forty days later after His ascension as Acts 2 records.

In understanding Jesus' discourse, we need to determine and be clear as to what "age" He was referring. To properly interpret the passage nothing must be "assumed" but the interpretation has to be based on the evidence in the discourse and on all pertinent scriptures.

The Old Testament period is stated as being 490 years in Daniel's prophecy of Daniel 9:24-27. Note what Daniel stated, "Seventy weeks are determined upon thy people and upon thy holy city, to finish the transgression, and to make an end of sins, and to make reconciliation for iniquity, and to bring in everlasting righteousness, and to seal up the vision and prophecy, and to anoint the most Holy." (Daniel 9:24)

The Jews were in Babylon in captivity and they were concerned about Israel's future and the fulfillment of God's promises to them. (V24) Daniel's prophecy was God's assurance that He was not finished with them and would accomplish His purpose for them. This prophecy stated that in 490 years God would restore their Kingdom and the Messiah would reign. This would end Israel's transgression, put an end their sins, make reconciliation for iniquity, and bring everlasting righteousness. Daniel foretold the period would end with "the vision and prophecy sealed", meaning accomplished, and the *most Holy*, the Messiah, would be anointed, referring to the Second Coming and His subsequent setting up of the Kingdom. All these events will end in the final days of the Old Testament dispensation which is Daniel's 70th week.

The "age" the disciples were asking about was the end of the Old Testament period when God would restore Israel under their Messiah. Many falsely conclude that the age Jesus is talking about involves the Church Age, and that He was addressing New Testament believers. However, the context and statements Jesus made negate that being the case. The age He speaks of here is the end of the Old Testament dispensation which is finalized at the end of the Seven Year Tribulation. The seven years will end the Old Testament dispensation with the Second Coming of Jesus the Messiah and His fulfilling His promises to them. Currently, today we are in an interval period that is our present Church Age, which is sandwiched in between the end of Daniel's 483 years and before Daniel's 70th Week. Israel was a nation which is distinctively different from a local New Testament church. This will be explained in detail later.

Christians in this Age are the Body and Bride of Christ

Clearly Christians are not present or mentioned in the Tribulation events of Matthew 24-25, nor in Revelation 4-19. Christians in the present age relate to the seven years, but Jesus' discourse is not addressing them. Yes, an innumerable number of people will be saved during the Tribulation which will include Jews and Gentiles (Matt. 24:14). But these saved people will be the last of the Old Testament saints saved, and not Christians who are the body of Christ. The New Testament repeatedly establishes this truth:

"Now ye are the body of Christ, and members in particular." (1 Corinthians 12:27)

"For the body is not one member, but many. If the foot shall say, Because I am not the hand, I am not of the body; is it therefore not of the body? And if the ear shall say, Because I am not the eye, I am not of the body; is it therefore not of the body? If the whole body were an eye, where were the hearing? If the whole were hearing, where were the smelling? But now hath God set the members every one of them in the body, as it hath pleased him. And if they were all one member, where were the body?

But now are they many members, yet but one body." (1 Corinthians 12:14-20)

"So we, being many, are one body in Christ, and every one members one of another." (Romans 12:5)

"Which is his body, the fulness of him that filleth all in all." (Ephesians 1:23)

"And he gave some, apostles; and some, prophets; and some, evangelists; and some, pastors and teachers; For the perfecting of the saints, for the work of the ministry, for the edifying of the body of Christ:" (Ephesians 4:11-12)

"For we are members of his body, of his flesh, and of his bones." (Ephesians 5:30)

"Who now rejoice in my sufferings for you, and fill up that which is behind of the afflictions of Christ in my flesh for his body's sake, which is the church:" (Colossians 1:24)

"For as we have many members in one body, and all members have not the same office:" (Romans 12:4)

Israel is never referred to as Christ's body. The body of Christ is unique to the believers in this Church Age. Further, believers in this dispensation are referred to in Revelation as the Bride of Christ.

"And there came unto me one of the seven angels which had the seven vials full of the seven last plagues, and talked with me, saying, Come hither, I will shew thee the bride, the Lamb's wife." (Revelation 21:9)

"And the Spirit and the bride say, Come. And let him that heareth say, Come. And let him that is athirst come. And whosoever will, let him take the water of life freely." (Revelation 22:17)

The rapture will end the present Church Age and when the seven-year Tribulation begins God will once again begin His prophetic clock and finalized Daniel's 490 years. Nothing in the New Testament, when properly interpreted, can be understood as placing Christians of this present dispensation within the Tribulation. The Tribulation is a Jewish event. However, the Bible is clear that many Gentiles will be saved during the period having believed on Jesus Christ. They will be saved Old Testament saints, but not part of the Body of Christ.

Prophetically there is no prophecy given to Christians about the end of the Church Age other than it will end with the rapture of believers. (1 Thess. 4:13-18) As will be shown, Christians are to be looking for the imminent return of the Savior and not signs.

I do not use the term the "rapture of the church" which implies that there is a universal church that Christ takes to heaven. God's plan in this the Church Age is an "ekklesia", (assembly or congregation) meaning a visible assembly of believers meeting in a specific geographical location. If one uses the term "rapture of the church, " he is saying churches will be raptured. What the New Testament teaches is that individual true believers who attend local assemblies will be raptured individually, not assemblies. (For an explanation of this truth go to https://www.bible-truth.org/Ekklesia.html, "The Translation of the Greek Word "Ekklesia" as "church" in the English Bible, and the use of the Term "the church" and its Ramifications.")

The Events of the Seven Year Tribulation are the End of the Old Testament Dispensation

Matthew 24-25 addresses the events of the seven-year Tribulation, which is the final seven years of Daniel's prophesy, and states that the Messiah would come and reign in power for 490 years. Jesus' ministry, as the Gospels record, was in the Old Testament dispensation. So far in time only 483 years of Daniel's prophecy has transpired which leaves the final seven years (Daniel's 70th Week) still future. During the 483rd year Daniel said the Messiah would be cut off, "And after threescore and two weeks shall Messiah be cut off, but not for himself: . . ." (Daniel 9:26) Jesus was crucified and that stopped God's prophetic clock from moving forward to His bringing in the promised kingdom to Israel. The remaining seven years will be completed in the seven-year Tribulation. Note the remainder of the verse and verse 27 describe the actions of the Antichrist which complete the 490 years.

Today clearly the Old Testament dispensation is not completed, but it will be ended with the coming of the Messiah at the end of the last week. Thus, none of the statements in Matthew 24-25 refer to the Church Age or Church Age saints

(Christians). It relates to Israel and God's promises to them.

To help our understanding of these saints the following is from your author's commentary on the Book of Revelation, Chapter 7:9-17

"John sees ". . . a great multitude, which no man could number, of all nations, and kindreds, and people, and tongues, stood before the throne, and before the Lamb, clothed with white robes, and palms in their hands;" (Rev. 7:9) In this heavenly scene, the saints of God are praising the Lord with the angels, the elders, and the four beasts, who fall down before the Lord on their faces and worship Him. These together honor the Lord saying, "Saying, Amen: Blessing, and glory, and wisdom, and thanksgiving, and honor, and power, and might, be unto our God for ever and ever. Amen." (Revelation 7:12)

But who are these saints of God? Verse 13 states, "And one of the elders answered, saying unto me, What are these which are arrayed in white robes? and whence came they?" (Revelation 7:13) The verse records that one of the elders asks John, who are these arrayed in white robes, and where did they come from. The identity of the elders is not revealed, but obviously is one of the twenty-four elders of Revelation 4 who is most likely a Church Age saint. It is imperative that one understands fully, what is the question the elder asked. It appears this Church Age saint is wondering who are these saints and importantly, when they were .saved, because this saint, now in heaven, was raptured when all believers on the earth were taken to be with the Lord. These saints, the elder sees were not raptured with him, not being a part of the Church Age.

The answer establishes the identity of this great multitude of saints in heaven who are serving the Lord before the throne. The elder then identifies them as Tribulation saints. Revelation 7:14 states, as those who come out of the great tribulation. Note the words "great tribulation" is not capitalized. ". . . These are they which came out of great tribulation, and have washed their robes, and made them white in the blood of the Lamb." These saints believed in Jesus Christ after the rapture during the Tribulation. Clearly, they are those saved who come out of the great tribulation that has occurred on earth and have been martyred. The great tribulation the elder mentions refers to the persecution by the Antichrist. These are Tribulation saints who were slain, prior to this point in the Tribulation. In time, they are seen as Revelation 6:9-11 records, in heaven at the opening of the Fifth Seal.

"And they cried with a loud voice, saying, How long, O Lord, holy and true, dost thou not judge and avenge our blood on them that dwell on the earth? And white robes were given unto every one of them; and it was said unto them, that they should rest yet for a little season, until their fellowservants also and their brethren, that should be killed as they were, should be fulfilled." (Revelation 6:10-11)

These are saints still alive on earth who are awaiting martyrdom. It must be understood that Revelation 7 is a parenthetical section added within the chronology of the Book of Revelation. This Chapter reveals the sealing of the 144,000 and explains further the details of what John saw in Chapter 6 of the saints who have been martyred up to this point in the Tribulation and who are in heaven at the throne of God. Chapter 7 does not move the timing of the events of this period forward, but explains what will be going on behind the scenes.

As stated earlier, these are not believers of the present Church Age, but those who are saved and martyred since the beginning of the Tribulation and before the Fifth Seal. They cannot represent Church Age saints because all saints of this present age have not been martyred. Matthew 24:21records this was not just ordinary tribulation or persecution. This phrase establishes the magnitude of the "great tribulation" as being "... *such as was not since the beginning of the world to this time, no, nor ever shall be.*" Revelation 7:14, specifically states, these saints came out of great tribulation. All believers in the Church Age have not had to endure "great tribulation." These saints are not Church Age Christians, who are in heaven since the rapture; and surely died in the beginning of the seven years Tribulation.

When John penned this Book there were no chapter or verse divisions. It at first may appear that these are two different groups or times. But Chapter 7 is an extension of Chapter 6. This group is made up from many ethnic and geographical areas of the earth. These appear to be Jews and have "palms" in their hand, which may refer to the Feast of the Tabernacles when Israel rejoiced in the blessings of God. (Lev. 23:40-43) It's more pictures Jesus' Triumphant Entry into Jerusalem when the Lord presented Himself as Israel's Messiah. (See John 12:13)

Note that these people are saved and their sins washed white in the <u>blood of the Lamb as are all who believe in Jesus Christ</u>. There are two ways to look at this passage. First, Revelation 7:16 indicates these could have been physically thirsty and hungry while on earth, but were no longer, now being in heaven. This gives further indication that these lived in the first part of the Tribulation as there will be a famine as Revelation 6:6-8 explains. The reference to relief from the heat of the sun may refer to the sun's powerful rays causing great distress on earth and possibly partly causing the famine. Revelation 7:17 makes it very clear, as terrible as the Tribulation had been, it was now over for them and these saints now rest for all eternity in the presence of God. And He *". . . shall wipe away all tears from their eyes."*

Secondly, this could refer to these people being spiritually thirsty and hungry. This will be a terrible time on earth and men will faint under the stress and physical trauma of the Tribulation. When people are under such dire pressure some also seek spiritual relief to endure their trouble. I believe both apply.

Think about those who still remain on earth. Most people, still alive on earth in these terrible times, will be rejecting Christ. It is my opinion that one can surmise from this passage that most people who are saved, come to Christ in the first half of the Tribulation seeking God's help. Those remaining, in spite of all they have seen God do, will be rejecting Him. They could be saved if they would believe, but because of their hard hearts full of prideful sin and rebellion, they will suffer under the judgment and condemnation of their sin. Note Jesus' statement in John 3:19-20 *"And this is the condemnation, that light is come into the world, and men loved darkness rather than light, because their deeds were evil. For every one that doeth evil hateth the light, neither cometh to the light, lest his deeds should be reproved."* (John 3:19-20)

It is explained "Therefore are they before the throne of God, and serve him day and night in his temple: and he that sitteth on the throne shall dwell among them." (Rev. 7:15) He makes it plain that the blessings these saints will receive are related to the coming Millennial reign of Christ which follows the Tribulation. In the Millennial temple, these Tribulation saints with Church Age saints, will serve Christ continually both day and night. This and other passages of

Scripture indicate that the saints of God will not be idle in the Kingdom of God, but will have specific duties and be used in carrying out Christ's Kingdom. Paul said that Christians would judge angels. (1 Corinthians 6:3) Apparently, Church Age saints will serve the Lord in the thousand years by judging those living in the Millennium in their natural bodies. They administer the government for the thousand years.

Because this event follows the calling of the 144,000, these are probably those won to the Lord by the Jewish evangelists and those who were saved after witnessing the rapture. Today, many people who are not saved are familiar with the coming rapture and seeing it occur many will believe and be saved. Further, in verse 14, this is confirmed when John asks who are these rejoicing saints and he is told they are the ones who came out of great tribulation. The grammatical structure of this phrase shows that for this great multitude of saint's salvation for them has been accomplished. Their faith in the promises of God of salvation has borne its fruit and they are now safe in heaven with the Lord."[1]

---

[1] Cooper P. Abrams, III, A Commentary of the Book of Revelation, *The Revelation of Jesus Christ,* (http://bible-truth.org/Revelation-Chapter 7.html), 2013

Israel Will Be Restored by God

There is no question that the focus of Tribulation is a Jewish event when God will bring the Jews home, restore Israel as a nation, establish them in their promised Kingdom. God's promises are sure:

"Therefore fear thou not, O my servant Jacob, saith the LORD; neither be dismayed, O Israel: for, lo, I will save thee from afar, and thy seed from the land of their captivity; and Jacob shall return, and shall be in rest, and be quiet, and none shall make him afraid. For I am with thee, saith the LORD, to save thee: though I make a full end of all nations whither I have scattered thee, yet will I not make a full end of thee: but I will correct thee in measure, and will not leave thee altogether unpunished." (Jeremiah 30:10-11)

"And it shall come to pass in that day, that the Lord shall set his hand again the second time to recover the remnant of his people, which shall be left, from Assyria, and from Egypt, and from Pathros, and from Cush, and from Elam, and from Shinar, and from Hamath, and from the islands of the sea. And he shall set up an ensign for the nations, and shall assemble the outcasts of Israel, and gather together the dispersed of Judah from the four corners of the earth." (Isaiah 11:11-12)

"Since thou wast precious in my sight, thou hast been honourable, and I have loved thee: therefore will I give men for thee, and people for thy life. Fear not: for I am with thee: I will bring thy seed from the east, and gather thee from the west; I will say to the north, Give up; and to the south, Keep not back: bring my sons from far, and my daughters from the ends of the earth; Even every one that is called by my name: for I have created him for my glory, I have formed him; yea, I have made him." (Isaiah 43:4-7)

"Therefore, behold, the days come, saith the LORD, that it shall no more be said, The LORD liveth, that brought up the children of Israel out of the land of Egypt; But, The LORD liveth, that brought up the children of Israel from the land of the north, and from all the lands whither he had driven them: and I will bring them again into their land that I gave unto their fathers." (Jeremiah 16:14-15)

"And so all Israel shall be saved: as it is written, There shall come out of Sion the Deliverer, and shall turn away ungodliness from Jacob:" (Romans 11:26)

THE OLIVET DISCOURSE

Also see: Jer. 23:3-8, 26:14; Eze. 11:16-17, 28:25-26, 34:12-14, 37:21-22, 39:25-29; Amos 9:11-15; Zech. 8:4-8.

Many have concluded that on May 14, 1948 Israel became a nation and this was fulfilled prophecy. However, as marvelous as was, and Israel once again becoming a nation, what was created was a civil or secular nation who does not serve God and who have not accepted their Messiah. Modern Israel is not the Promised Land. The prophecy of Israel's restoration is specific in that when God restores and brings them back to their land, <u>but then will serve Him</u>. What has occurred today does not fulfill the prophecy of Israel's restoration. It should be seen only as a precursor of God setting the stage for Daniel's 70th week.

Israel's emphasis today is in having a place for the Jews to live as a nation and not about serving or honoring God. Even the orthodox Jews, who make up a large part of their population practice a false Judaism, following Talmud that is the writing of their rabbis instead of the Bible. Their religion, Judaism is a works for salvation theology and has little to do with biblical teaching.

THE OLIVET DISCOURSE

However, when God makes them a nation, the Jews in the beginning of the Tribulation, they will in mass return to Israel and they will begin to serve the Lord. It is God who makes them a nation. This is seen in the rebuilding the Temple and the restoration of the temple sacrifices. Today that is not occurring, but it will in the seven-year Tribulation. It is clear that when God brings the Jews back to Israel in the Tribulation is God's final appeal to Israel to believe and receive Him as their Messiah. (See Eze. 37:1-28) Many will believe and endure the persecutions of the Antichrist and be martyred.

During the beginning of the Tribulation, the Jews will rebuild their temple which will no doubt infuriate the Antichrist and Satan whom he serves. (Eze. 37:26-17) The Antichrist will show contempt for God and the Jews and declaring himself to be a god. He will set his statue in the Holy of Holies as did Antiochus Epiphanes as Daniel recorded, and require the Jews to worship him. (Dan. 9:27; Matt. 24:15-22) In his rage there will be wholesale murder of the Jews and all who worship Jesus Christ. These are the martyrs of Revelation 6-7. Further, there will be no peace in Israel until God brings it.

THE OLIVET DISCOURSE

We often hear the request to "pray for the peace of Jerusalem". It is a futile prayer in this dispensation of the Church Age. It should be understood there will be no peace in Jerusalem until Jesus returns at His second coming at the end of the seven-year Tribulation. Realistically, praying for the peace of Jerusalem is praying for the Lord Jesus to return.

God Will Give Israel Their Promised Kingdom

At His Second Coming the Lord will then fulfill His promises to the nation of Israel in what is referred to as the Promised Kingdom which we know is the coming Millennium (1000-year reign of Christ - Revelation 20:6). During the Tribulation, God purges the earth of sinners, preparing this world for His Millennial reign.

This was fully in the minds of Jesus' disciples when they ask Him. "When they therefore were come together, they asked of him, saying, Lord, wilt thou at this time restore again the kingdom to Israel?" (Acts 1:6)

What Kingdom? The Kingdom God promised the Jews. God said: "At that time they shall call Jerusalem the throne of the LORD; and all the nations shall be gathered unto it, to the name of the LORD, to Jerusalem: neither shall they walk any more after the imagination of their evil heart." (Jeremiah 3:17)

"Then will I sprinkle clean water upon you, and ye shall be clean: from all your filthiness, and from all your idols, will I cleanse you. A new heart also will I give you, and a new spirit will I put within you: and I will take away the stony heart out of your flesh, and I will give you a heart of flesh. And I will put my spirit within you, and cause you to walk in my statutes, and ye shall keep my judgments, and do them. And ye shall dwell in the land that I gave to your fathers; and ye shall be my people, and I will be your God." (Ezekiel 36:25-28)

The parallels the accounts in Mark 13:1f and Luke 21:5f tells us that Jesus' discourse of Matthew 24-25 occurred just after Jesus had left the temple for the last time and had predicted its destruction. He said that not one stone of this magnificent temple structure would be left upon another. (See Luke 21:5) Can there be any doubt that the disciples perceived that because of the degree of destruction that would destroy the temple, that Jesus was referring to events at the end of their present age and the coming of the promised Kingdom? Jerusalem and the temple were destroyed in 70 A.D which is also evidence that the Old Testament dispensation was postponed.

The age the disciples referred to is the end of the Old Testament dispensation which would end in God restoring the nation of Israel, establishing their Promised Kingdom, and their Messiah ruling from Jerusalem. This present age in which we are living today is a different age that we refer to as the Church Age.

The Misinterpretation of Matthew 16:18-18

At the time Jesus responded to the disciples' question, the current Church Age was not in view and did not begin until fifty days after Christ returned to Heaven. Many scholars believe that Jesus predicted the Church Age in His statement found in Matthew 16:18, "And I say also unto thee, That thou art Peter, and upon this rock I will build my church; (*ekklesia*) and the gates of hell shall not prevail against it. And I will give unto thee the keys of the kingdom of heaven: and whatsoever thou shalt bind on earth shall be bound in heaven: and whatsoever thou shalt loose on earth shall be loosed in heaven." (Matthew 16:19)" (Matthew 16:18)

Jesus was speaking to Jews, and if one is consistent in following the rules of interpretation, it must be considered He said Peter's confession was the basis of the "kingdom of heaven." <u>I do not think Jesus was referring to the Church Age. The "ekklesia" Jesus was building was the prelude for the promised kingdom, not a "church" or assembly of believers.</u> The "assembly" Jesus was referring to would be made up of those Jews that believed on Jesus Christ as their Messiah. In verse 20, Jesus

THE OLIVET DISCOURSE

charged his disciple not to tell others He was the Christ (Messiah).

That is consistent with verses 18-19 referring to the kingdom. Clearly, that is what Jesus actually said. The disciples as well as most of the Jews, were looking for God to fulfill His promises to Israel and were asking when the Messiah would return and set up His promised Kingdom. Christ's strong condemnation of the scribes and Pharisees of Matthew 23 clearly set the stage for the disciples to be very concerned about these events. Jesus said that judgment would come upon this generation (Matt. 23:36-39). The judgment came in 70 A.D. when Judaism was destroyed and the Jews dispersed over the known world.

Let me reiterate, that in Matthew 24:2, Jesus said that the beautiful Jewish temple, where they were standing, would be completely destroyed. This was shocking news to the disciples and greatly alarming to them. Judaism was centered in worship in the temple. Jesus then left the temple grounds proceeding east. He exited probably walking across the Kidron Valley to the Mount of Olives, which was in sight of the City of David.

As He sat on the Mount of Olives, the disciples came to Him privately as Matthew 24:3 records, and ask Him when these things would occur and what would be the signs of the end of the age.

Surely, they were also troubled by Jesus' statement in Matthew 26:2, "Ye know that after two days is *the feast of* the passover, and the Son of man is betrayed to be crucified." (Matthew 26:2) They had followed the Lord Jesus for three years and were clearly disturbed that He said He would be crucified. Probably, they wondered if He would be killed by crucifixion, how could He bring about the promised kingdom?

Can we stop here for a moment and consider that in the Gospels, Jesus ministry was directed at presenting to Israel their promised kingdom. Jesus in Matthew 4:23, 9:35 preaching the Gospel of the Kingdom.

"And Jesus went about all Galilee, teaching in their synagogues, and preaching the gospel of the kingdom, and healing all manner of sickness and all manner of disease among the people.' (Matthew 4:23)

"And Jesus went about all the cities and villages, teaching in their synagogues, and preaching the gospel of the kingdom, and healing every sickness and every disease among the people." (Matthew 9:35)

Never in the Gospels is the current Church Age in view. It was about Israel and God's promises to them that was the Messiah come to establish God's kingdom of Israel. The point here is that contextually, the question that Jesus answered in the Olivet Discourse and the subject of His discourse was the end of the age (*aion*) and the coming of His promised Kingdom.

The disciples did not know anything about the coming Church Age or institution of the local church. Therefore, Jesus's statements were not about this present age, but rather addressing the end of the Old Testament dispensation. Certainly, believers of this present age will be a part of the Kingdom, but only through their relationship as the bride of Christ. They will also be serving Christ as He rules the Kingdom. A bride becomes the bridegrooms "helpmeet." Paul spoke of this to Timothy saying "Therefore I endure all things for the elect's sakes, that they may also obtain the salvation which is in Christ Jesus with eternal glory. It is a faithful saying: For if we be dead with him, we shall also live with him: If we suffer, we shall also reign with him: if we deny him, he also will deny us:" (2 Timothy 2:10-12) Paul uses the pronouns "we, us" which are clearly Christians in this age which began at Pentecost in Acts 2.

To the Corinthians, Paul wrote "Do ye not know that the saints shall judge the world? and if the world shall be judged by you, are ye unworthy to judge the smallest matters? Know ye not that we shall judge angels? how much more things that pertain to this life? If then ye have judgments of things pertaining to this life, set them to judge who are least esteemed in the church." (1 Corinthians 6:2-4) This was written to Christians in the Church Age. When will they judge the world and angels? Without question it will be in the coming Millennial reign of Christ.

Jesus was Preparing His Disciples for His Return to Heaven

Permit me to labor the point. Many times, before, Jesus had explained to the disciples that He would be killed and would be leaving them. For example, in Matthew 16:21-28, Jesus told His disciples He would be killed, and be raised from the dead on the third day. (See Matt. 14:1f, 26:2; John 13:33) These statements about His death and ascension preceded Matthew 24 and had set the stage for the uneasiness of the disciples concerning future events. They were looking for Him as the Messiah to set up the Kingdom, but He had not explained to them how this would be done. Thus, as stated earlier, contextually the Olivet Discourse is related to the Jews and Jesus is addressing the coming promised Kingdom which would begin with the Daniel's 70th Week (the Seven Year Tribulation) and His Second Coming. He plainly states this in Matthew 24:15, "When ye therefore shall see the abomination of desolation, spoken of by Daniel the prophet, stand in the holy place, (whoso readeth, let him understand:)" (Matthew 24:15, Mark 13:14) The "they" are Tribulation saints. The present Church Age is not in view here. What is in view are Daniel's prophecies:

"And after threescore and two weeks shall Messiah be cut off, but not for himself: and the people of the prince that shall come shall destroy the city and the sanctuary; and the end thereof shall be with a flood, and unto the end of the war desolations are determined. And he shall confirm the covenant with many for one week: and in the midst of the week he shall cause the sacrifice and the oblation to cease, and for the overspreading of abominations he shall make it desolate, even until the consummation, and that determined shall be poured upon the desolate." (Daniel 9:26-27)

Note that in Matthew 24:14, the Gospel that is being referred to as the "<u>Gospel of the Kingdom</u>." Matthew 3:2, 4:17, 10:5-7, records that John the Baptist, and Jesus both preached the "*Kingdom of God is at hand.*" Throughout Jesus' ministry, this was the Gospel He preached. The Good News presented to the Jews proclaimed the coming Kingdom and that He was the promised Messiah.

The Jews clearly understood that the coming of the Messiah would bring about the promised Kingdom Age of the Nation of Israel. The term "Gospel of the Kingdom" is only found four times in the New Testament and only in the four Gospels. (Mt 4:23; Mt 9:35; Mt 24:14; Mr 1:14) The word "gospel" is found eighty-one times in the rest of the

THE OLIVET DISCOURSE

New Testament without the mention of the kingdom. The other sixty-two books of the New Testament are about the Church Age or the "ekklesia" and not about the promised Kingdom to the Jews. The disciples understood that the Old Testament prophets had foretold this Kingdom, and the Jews had been longing for it for centuries, because it promised them to bring them the peace, security, prosperity, righteousness that God had promised them.

In the New Testament, Jesus is referred to as Christ, which is the Greek word of Messiah. Father, He is called our Savior, the Son of God, and numerous other titles, but not to Church Age believers as their Messiah. Jesus is only referred to as the Messiah in the Gospel and never in the rest of the New Testament.

The Kingdom of Heaven Presented and Temporarily Withdrawn

Today, Christians are not longing for a kingdom, but the soon return of our Savior at the rapture and of being with Him in heaven. The gospel of the Kingdom that Jesus preached was of the coming Kingdom and is not the same as the Gospel of the Church Age which presents salvation based on the death, burial and resurrection of the Lord Jesus Christ to all men, Jews and Gentiles alike. Jesus was presenting the promised Kingdom to Israel when He would sit on the throne of David and rule the world from Jerusalem.

Isaiah prophesied of this saying, "For unto us a child is born, unto us a son is given: and the government shall be upon his shoulder: and his name shall be called Wonderful, Counseller, The mighty God, The everlasting Father, The Prince of Peace. Of the increase of his government and peace there shall be no end, upon the throne of David, and upon his kingdom, to order it, and to establish it with judgment and with justice from henceforth even for ever. The zeal of the LORD of hosts will perform this." (Isaiah 9:6-7)

Israel's entrance into the Kingdom would be clearly based on their accepting Him as their Messiah, and their spiritual rebirth as Jesus made clear in John 3:3. Nicodemus believed that his Jewish heritage and good works were the prerequisite for his being in the kingdom. He told Nicodemus ". . . Verily, verily, I say unto thee, Except a man be born again, he cannot see the kingdom of God." (John 3:3)

John 3:15-16 also are directed toward Nicodemus and the Jews. Yes, it is also given to us in the Church Age and is relevant to both Jews and Gentiles. However, contextually it at this time was focused on the Jews. Note that verse 14 refers to the event in Israel's history when Moses lifted up the serpent in Numbers 21:8-9.

The Christians of this age who believe and accept Jesus Christ as their Savior are spiritually reborn, have their sins forgiven, and receive eternal life. However, their place in God's plan is not to inherit the Kingdom "per se." Their place in the Kingdom is to be Christ's bride and body, and as a part of the Kingdom, ruling with Him. (Dan. 7:22; 1 Cor. 6:2; Rev. 1:6; 5:10, 20:4).

Comparing the Good News for Israel and to Christians in This Age

Jesus and John the Baptist preached the Good News of the offer of the Kingdom. John's Gospel was ". . . Repent ye: for the kingdom of heaven is at hand." (Matthew 3:2) Jesus also preached the same message, "From that time Jesus began to preach, and to say, Repent: for the kingdom of heaven is at hand." (Matthew 4:17) Jesus was the King, and He was proclaiming Himself as the Messiah and offering Israel their promised Kingdom.

Note the comparison between Matthew 24:14, with 1 Cor. 15:1 4.

"And this gospel of the kingdom shall be preached in all the world for a witness unto all nations; and then shall the end come." (Matthew 24:14) (Also see Matt. 4:23, 9:35, 24:14; Mark 1:14-15) Note, that contextually this will occur during the Tribulation. In reality, although the Gospel today is being preached around the world, it is not being preached "unto all nations." The 144,000 Jewish missionaries and Tribulation saints will be the ones who proclaim the Gospel to all nations.

THE OLIVET DISCOURSE

Understand that Jesus said it was the Gospel (Good News) of the kingdom.

This is the Gospel that Paul preached in our age as we believers today, "Moreover, brethren, I declare unto you the gospel which I preached unto you, which also ye have received, and wherein ye stand; By which also ye are saved, if ye keep in memory what I preached unto you, unless ye have believed in vain. For I delivered unto you first of all that which I also received, how that Christ died for our sins according to the scriptures; And that he was buried, and that he rose again the third day according to the scriptures:" (1 Corinthians 15:1-4)

"But the Lord said unto him, Go thy way: for he is a chosen vessel unto me, to bear my name before the Gentiles, and kings, and the children of Israel:" (Acts 9:15)

"And when Silas and Timotheus were come from Macedonia, Paul was pressed in the spirit, and testified to the Jews that Jesus was Christ. And when they opposed themselves, and blasphemed, he shook his raiment, and said unto them, <u>Your blood be upon your own heads; I am clean: from henceforth I will go unto the Gentiles</u>." (Acts 18:5-6) [Emphasis added]

THE OLIVET DISCOURSE

Those that "opposed themselves" were the unbelieving Jews who, without question, violently rejected Jesus as their Messiah and sought repeatedly to murder Paul. This was the turning point in Paul's ministry. Paul, seeing the Jews utter rejection of Jesus turned to the Gentiles to whom God had called him to preach. (Acts 9:15-16, 20:25-26) He abandoned going to the synagogues and from this point on peached Christ to the Gentiles.

The Book of Acts Reveals the Transition from the Kingdom Offered to Israel to the Present Church Age

It is vital to understand the transition that the Gospels record that Jesus was offering them the promised kingdom that He will establish in the Millennium. Jesus, after His resurrection set the stage for the offer of the Kingdom in Acts 1:3-8. Jesus instructed His disciples, "To whom also he shewed himself alive after his passion by many infallible proofs, being seen of them forty days, and <u>speaking of the things pertaining to the kingdom of God</u>:" (Acts 1:3) [Emphasis added]

Had the nation believed and received the Lord Jesus as their Messiah, the last years of the Old Testament dispensation would have continued with the seven-year Tribulation, and ending with His Second Coming. However, the Jews did not believe and the nation rejected Christ. God's offer of the salvation of Israel and the Kingdom thus was withdrawn and will remain withdrawn until the seven-year Tribulation. Jews who are saved today become part of the bride and the body of Jesus Christ and will be raptured with all believers of this age.

THE OLIVET DISCOURSE

Peter also boldly preached that Jesus was the promised Messiah. "Therefore let all the house of Israel know assuredly, that God hath made that same Jesus, whom ye have crucified, both Lord and Christ." (Acts 2:36) Note what Jesus told Peter when the Lord announced, ". . . That thou art Peter, and upon this rock I will build my church; and the gates of hell shall not prevail against it. And I will give unto thee the keys of the kingdom of heaven: and whatsoever thou shalt bind on earth shall be bound in heaven: and whatsoever thou shalt loose on earth shall be loosed in heaven." (Matthew 16:18-19) Peter was given the keys to <u>the kingdom of heaven, which</u> was the saving message that Jesus was the Messiah who would ". . . save His people from their sins" as the angel proclaimed to Joseph." (Matt. 1:21) The phrase "his people" is a reference to Israel.

Peter did not start a universal ekklesia (church) as the Roman Catholic Church falsely claims. The ekklesia (church, assembly) Jesus said He would build was on Peter's confession of Jesus being the Son of God and the Christ (Matt. 16:20) Peter was not a pope on which a church was built, but a faithful Apostle of Jesus Christ and a gospel preacher.

It must be understood that Paul initially preached the Gospel to the Jews. "For I am not ashamed of the gospel of Christ: for it is the power of God unto salvation to every one that believeth; to the Jew first, and also to the Greek." (Romans 1:16)

Why did he say to the "Jew first?" Because at this time Israel was still being offered salvation through Jesus Christ. The Jews were still a nation. The Jews that did believe became members of Christ's body. God was still giving Israel the chance to be saved even though they were not being offered the kingdom. Those that believed at Pentecost became part of the Church Age and were indwelled by the Holy Spirit and are at this moment, enjoying heaven and at the rapture will become the Bride of Christ. In Acts 10:45, Cornelius, the Roman Centurion, after Peter explained the Gospel to him, believed and received the Holy Ghost meaning he became a Christian, indwelled by the Holy Spirit, and a member of the body of Christ. Lydia also in Acts 16:14-15, was a Jew and was worshiping God. When she met Paul and he explained the gospel she was baptized as a Christian.

This does not mean that if the Jews believed and accepted Jesus as their Messiah, He would not have had to be crucified. Paul plainly preached to the Jews that Jesus had to suffer and be crucified. At this time Paul was preaching in the synagogues. In emphasizing that Jesus was not only the Savoir but the Christ (Messiah) To the Thessalonians he proclaimed, "Opening and alleging, that Christ must needs have suffered, and risen again from the dead; and that this Jesus, whom I preach unto you, is Christ." (Acts 17:3) (Also see Heb: 6:23-28) Christ's suffering, death, and resurrection was the basis of salvation and the foundation of God's offer to Israel of the Kingdom.

However, the Jews refused to accept their Messiah and plotted to kill Paul. It was at this time, as previously stated, that God began to at that time to withdraw the offer of the kingdom. In 70 A.D., when the Romans destroyed Jerusalem and dispersed the Jews, Israel as a nation no longer existed and that period lasts even until today. Modern Israel in not the Promised Kingdom. This can be seen as the final act in the Lord postponing the Kingdom. It must be appreciated that although the offer of the Kingdom was withdrawn, it was only a temporary secession of the offer. The Old Testament abounds with prophecies of God restoring Israel and given them a kingdom. This is the Millennial Kingdom that will follow the Tribulation and Second Coming.

THE OLIVET DISCOURSE

In the Book of Acts records God's bona fide salvation to Israel. The New Testament records the Lord Jesus Christ gathering to Himself also a bride and body from the Gentiles. Thus, the Book of Acts unfolds a transitional period in which God was offering salvation to the Jews. All believers Immedicably after Pentecost were Jews, but by the end of the 1st Century the churches were mostly made up of saved Gentiles.

"And when they had appointed him a day, there came many to him into *his* lodging; to whom he expounded and testified the kingdom of God, persuading them concerning Jesus, both out of the law of Moses, and *out of* the prophets, from morning till evening. And some believed the things which were spoken, and some believed not. And when they agreed not among themselves, they departed, after that Paul had spoken one word, Well spake the Holy Ghost by Esaias the prophet unto our fathers, Saying, Go unto this people, and say, Hearing ye shall hear, and shall not understand; and seeing ye shall see, and not perceive: For the heart of this people is waxed gross, and their ears are dull of hearing, and their eyes have they closed; lest they should see with *their* eyes, and hear with *their* ears, and understand with *their* heart, and should be converted, and I should heal them. <u>Be it known therefore unto you, that the salvation of God</u>

is sent unto the Gentiles, and *that* they will hear it." (Acts 28:23-28)

<u>Because so many have ignored and not understood this truth, there has been a flood of misinterpretation and confusion by those who mix God's plans for the Jews with that of Christians in the Church Age.</u> Because of the lack of a discerning of the times there is presently a rash of false teaching that distorts the truths of salvation, eschatology, ecclesiology, and God's plan for believers in the Church Age.

Many Christians are confused and there is great division. <u>THIS OUGHT NOT TO BE!</u> God has plainly revealed His truth, but sinful men, yes, even some well-meaning pastors, Bible scholars, and Christians, have failed to be true and faithful students of His word. "Study to shew thyself approved unto God, a workman that needeth not to be ashamed, rightly dividing the word of truth." (2 Timothy 2:15) Many should hang their heads in shame, confess their sin, learn, and preach God's truth.

Let no one make the mistake of thinking that God is finished with Israel. Scriptures abound with the Lord's promises to restore Israel that was previously referenced in this paper. The question

THE OLIVET DISCOURSE

needs to be asked and biblically understood; What is God's purpose for the Tribulation?

Unmistakably, God's purpose is to renew His offer of the Kingdom to Israel and subsequently save millions of Jews and Gentiles. In the end He purges the world of those that reject Him as their Messiah and God. This ushers in the Millennial reign of Jesus Christ, which was God's plan from the beginning. God will fulfill to the letter His promises to Israel.

As stressed in this discourse, Jesus did not offer the Millennial Kingdom to Christians in our dispensation, although Church Age saints certainly will be a part of it. Christians are given something much better, which is being a part of the Body of Christ and His bride who will rule with Him in the Kingdom. The Old Testament saints were not permanently indwelt by the Holy Spirit and the Tribulation saints, being a part of the final days of the Old Testament period will logically not be indwelled either. The Holy Spirit will be active bring conviction and filling the lives of these saints, but not permanently indwelling them.

Christians In the Church Age Will Not Go into or Through Any Part of The Seven Year Tribulation. (Rev. 3:10)

Believers today have the promise of God that we will not go through the coming seven-year Tribulation. The Lord promised to those who keep His word, "Because thou hast kept the word of my patience, I also will keep thee from the hour of temptation, which shall come upon all the world, to try them that dwell upon the earth. (Revelation 3:10) This statement was made to the Philadelphian church that exists before the apostasy of the lukewarm Laodiceans.

Two important evidences show that the scope of the "the *hour of temptation*" is that It is a global event and involves the entire world. The word "world" is οικουμενη *oikoumene* which means the earth or globe. Second, the phrase "hour of temptation" is preceded by the article "the." If God had not used the article, the phrase could mean a general period of temptation, but with the article the period is specific. The Lord is not saying I will keep thee from a general period of temptation, but a specific period which is the seven-year Tribulation. Since Christ instituted the local church there have always been periods of persecutions and temptations of believers, wars, rumors of wars, apostasy, natural disasters that Christians have had to endure with the rest of the world. So, this statement is not referring to a general keeping from temptation, but a specific period which comes on all the earth. The question then is what period will bring a specific temptation on all the earth?

The answer is clear that the period is the coming seven-year Tribulation, because it will be a global event. Thus, the Lord is saying, I will keep you from that specific hour. How? The Lord will rapture Christians in this age and remove them before the Tribulation begins. This will end the Church Age. Believers in this the Church Age will not enter or go through any part of the Tribulation when God judges the world, and offers again to save Israel and give them their promised kingdom.

The Misinterpretation of 2 Thessalonians 2:1-4

In 2 Thessalonians 2:1-4 Paul wrote, "Now we beseech you, brethren, by the coming of our Lord Jesus Christ, and by our gathering together unto him, That ye be not soon shaken in mind, or be troubled, neither by spirit, nor by word, nor by letter as from us, as that the day of Christ is at hand. Let no man deceive you by any means: for that day shall not come, except there come a falling away first, and that man of sin be revealed, the son of perdition; Who opposeth and exalteth himself above all that is called God, or that is worshipped; so that he as God sitteth in the temple of God, shewing himself that he is God."

Those who teach a Pre, Mid, or Post Tribulational rapture use this as their proof text. They proclaim that Christians in the Church Age will go into the Tribulation, but not through the worst part of "that day" the of "day of Christ." They misunderstand and conclude that the 'day of Christ' is the same as the "day of the Lord." (Isa 2:12; Isa 13:6,9; Isa 34:8; Jer 46:10; La 2:22; Eze 13:5; Eze 30:3; Joe 1:15; Joe 2:1,11,31; Joe 3:14; Am 5:18,20; Ob 15; Zep 1:7-8,14,18; Zep 2:2-3; Zec 14:1; Mal 4:5; Ac 2:20; 1Co 5:5; 2Co 1:14; 1Th 5:2; 2 Pe 3:10) The "day of the Lord" is the day the time of judgment when God judges the sins of man. It happens during the seven-year Tribulation prior to His Second Coming. Further, it is the time when God will begin again His prophetic clock and once again offer Israel their promised kingdom. One evidence of this is the 144,000 Jews saved and sealed in the beginning of seven years, being twelve-thousand of each of the twelve tribes of Israel. (Rev. 7:4-12) Most believe this 144,000 will be Jewish evangelists who will preach the Gospel in every nation. (Matt. 24:14; Rev.14:6-7)

In other words, the Tribulation is the final seven years of Daniel's 490 "week" when the Lord will confirm His covenant with Israel and the Messiah will return and restore Jerusalem and set up the Millennial kingdom. (Dan. 9:15   They teach Christians will enter the first part of the "Jacob's trouble" (the Tribulation), but will be spared the worst of the seven years of Tribulation. Their error is in mixing God's specific promises to Israel with the believers in the Church Age, plus seeing "the church" as a universal institution which needs to be purified. In their thinking the first part of the Tribulation will be God "purifying" "the church." A church (ekklesia) is simply a group of professing individual believers. There are many who assemble in churches that are not born again. No scripture states that "churches" will be raptured.   If churches are to be purified, then each attendee or member must be purified by their faith in Jesus Christ and have their sins forgiven. (Eph. 2:8-10, Col. 2:14) Are not the true believers who attend churches already purified? (See 1 Cor. 6:11; Heb. 10:22, 1 Pet. 1:22, Rev. 1:5) Do they need to be "re-purified'?

On close examination and the idea that believers will go into the seven-year Tribulation is with the Scriptures and is completely in line with Revelation 3:10 and the Pre-Tributional return of Christ.

However, realistically there will be churches that enter the seven years, these worldly assemblies, cults, being false churches, whose members are not born again. These congregations and denominations teach a false gospel, and works for salvation and deny Jesus Christ by rejecting Him and His word.

To begin with, the passage is giving strong assurance to the Thessalonian believers that they had not missed the return of Christ which for Christians is the rapture. False teachers apparently had been teaching that the rapture had already taken place and they had missed it. There was persecution which the false teachers explained, indicated they were in the Tribulation. Paul says the "day of Christ" which refers to the rapture had not occurred; therefore, they had not missed the Lord's return.

The statement "is at hand" *enistemi*, in verse 2, is often misinterpreted and falsely assumed to say that it is the rapture that is not at hand or near. This would contradict the many scriptures that teach the imminent return of the Lord. However, the definition of the word "ενιστημι, *enistemi*, means "to be present" or is now present.[2] Thayer also lists the word as meaning "present."[3] Romans 8:38, 1 Corinthians 7:26, Galatians 1:4, Hebrews 9:9, 1 Cor. 3:22, all translate the word "ενιστημι" as "present." What Paul said to the Thessalonians was that the rapture was not present at that time and had not occurred. He continued and warned them not to let anyone deceive them because a falling away or apostasy must come first. This falling away and apostasy will occur during the Tribulation when God sends strong delusion and many believe the lies of the Antichrist. If the rapture had taken place the Thessalonians would

---

[2] W. E. Vines, An Expository Dictionary of New Testament Words (Nashville:Thomas Nelson, 1985) p.288.

[3] Joseph H. Thayer, Thayer's Greek-English Lexicon of the New Testament (Hendrickson:Mass, 2003).

have been in the Tribulation period, but clearly, they were not. The falling away and the advent of the Antichrist had not occurred. Thus, they were assured the rapture had not happened because they were not in the Tribulation.

The Imminent Return of Christ.

In the New Testament the Lord's return is always seen as imminent. Believers in this Church Age are to be ever ready for the rapture. If the rapture would take somewhere in the Tribulation, the any moment return of the Lord would lose its emphasis. If in the Tribulation, a Christian could read the Book of Revelation and accurately figure when it would take place by observing the predicted events of the various judgments. Further, the time frame could be calculated as to the Second Coming. It is interesting that among those who reject the Pre-Tribulational rapture there is no consensus as to when it will occur. Their views widely vary from sometime around the Sixth Seal until the Second Coming. A false interpretation always produces confusion.

Walvoord affirms the imminent return of the Lord, "Since the beginning of the early churches, believers have longed for the return of their Savior.

Repeatedly, the New Testament tells believers that the Lord's return is "at hand." This phrase uses the word εγγιζω *eggizo* which means "near or nigh."[4] The phrase is used 7 times in the New Testament. In Romans 13:12; Philippians 4:5; 1 Peter 4:7; 2 Timothy 4:6; Revelation 1:3, 22:10 and each uses the word *eggizo*. 2 Timothy 4:6 and 2 Thessalonians 2:2 use the word *enistemi*. Each reference is to the imminent return of the Lord. God is telling us in the age we are in that the rapture is always possible, being "at hand."

Paul encouraged Titus to be, "Looking for that blessed hope, and the glorious appearing of the great God and our Saviour Jesus Christ;" (Titus 2:13) Titus lived in the 1st Century, yet Paul told him to be looking for Christ's return and the rapture. He reminded them in 1 Thessalonians 4:4, "Therefore let us not sleep, as do others; but let us watch and be sober. For they that sleep sleep in the night; and they that be drunken are drunken in the night. But let us, who are of the day, be sober, putting on the breastplate of faith and love; and for a helmet, the hope of salvation. For God hath not appointed us to wrath, but to obtain salvation by our Lord Jesus Christ," (1 Thessalonians 5:6-9)

---

[4] Vines, p.288.

Paul encouraged the Thessalonians to be continually ready for the Lord's return, "And to wait for his Son from heaven, whom he raised from the dead, *even* Jesus, which delivered us from the wrath to come. (1 Thessalonians 1:10). The word "wait" is "ἀναμένω" and is in the present tense (a continuous action) meaning they were being told to look for the Lord's imminent return unceasingly. Further, there is never any sign said to precede the rapture.

In looking for the imminent return of Christ, Paul wrote Titus, "Teaching us that, denying ungodliness and worldly lusts, we should live soberly, righteously, and godly, in this present world; Looking for that blessed hope, and the glorious appearing of the great God and our Saviour Jesus Christ;" (Titus 2:12-13) The words "looking for" are in the present tense meaning believers in the early assemblies were to wait confidently and with patience for the rapture.

1 John 3:3 would have little significance if Christ's return was not imminent. "Beloved, now are we the sons of God, and it doth not yet appear what we shall be: but we know that, when he shall appear, we shall be like him; for we shall see him as he is. And every man that hath this hope in him purifieth himself, even as he is pure." (1 John 3:2-

3) John is speaking about the rapture when believers of this Church Age will be resurrected. Looking for Christ's imminent return is one incentive for a Christian to live a godly life daily for the Lord. To the Romans, Paul urged them to "wake up" because the return of the Lord was nearer than they thought. (See Rom. 13:11-14)

James, the Lord's half-brother, in the first book of the New Testament that was written to tell these early believers, "Be ye also patient; stablish your hearts: for the coming of the Lord draweth nigh. Grudge not one against another, brethren, lest ye be condemned: behold, the judge standeth before the door." (James 5:8-9) The phrase "Is at hand is *êggiken* which grammatically is the present perfect active indicative of *eggizô*, that is a common verb, meaning to "draw near." He was consoling them that those that persecuted them would face the judgment of God.

Further, Matthew 24:21-22, specifically states that Jesus is referring to the events of "great tribulation" and leaves no room for doubt as to the period Christ is describing. This was written to the Jews in the Tribulation evidenced by Jesus' reference to Daniel.

Another point is that the Lord did not use the term "the day of the Lord" which in the Old and New Testament is used 29 times and refers to a time of

God's judgment when He pours out His wrath on unbelievers.[5] Most of those who put the rapture in the Tribulation falsely conclude the phrase "day of Christ" is the same as "day of the Lord." However, the phrase here is "day of Christ" and refers to the rapture which is the "blessed hope" for Church Age saints. The "day of Christ" will be a time of rejoicing for Christians, not of sorrow and bitterness as "the day of the Lord" characterizes.

The phrase "day of the Lord" is used in 1 Thessalonians 5:2. "But of the times and the seasons, brethren, ye have no need that I write unto you. For yourselves know perfectly that the day of the Lord, so cometh as a thief in the night. For when they shall say, Peace and safety; then sudden destruction cometh upon them, as travail upon a woman with child; and they shall not escape. But ye, brethren, are not in darkness, that that day should overtake you as a thief. Ye are all the children of light, and the children of the day: we are not of the night, nor of darkness." (1 Thessalonians 5:1-5)

The term "times and season" is a reference to the signs of the coming events of the Tribulation and God's terrible events in "day of the Lord" when

---

[5] See Isaiah 13:9–11; Amos 5:18–20; 1 Thess 5:2–3; 2 Pet 3:10; Rev 6:17; 16:14.

THE OLIVET DISCOURSE

God will execute His judgment on the world. Christians are not told to look for signs. "For the Jews require a sign, and the Greeks seek after wisdom:" (1 Corinthians 1:22) Gentiles, which is a reference to non-Jews seek wisdom, meaning knowledge that is of course found in God's word.

Paul was addressing early believers was prophetically addressing the future. He was revealing God's plan for judgment on the ungodly in the same way we teach these truths today. Christians are not in the Tribulation and we will not experience God's wrath, but we are assured that God will execute His judgment on the sinful world that rejects His mercy and grace and follows Satan. This is a great consolation to God's children that one day He will judge the wicked and bring righteousness to the world.

To properly interpret the passage the phrase "day of the Lord" needs to be identified. First, Paul continues his explanation of the rapture and explains they have no need that he writes them concerning *the times and season.* He stresses the fact that the Lord's coming will not be announced and comes as a thief in the night. He emphasizes this point by showing the unsaved that are <u>not</u> looking for the imminent return of Christ will be suddenly faced with destruction and they shall not escape. These are unbelievers who reject the Gospel of Jesus Christ. The reference to the travail of a woman further illustrates the destruction comes suddenly and more importantly unavoidably. Those who are not ready for the rapture and have rejected Jesus Christ as their Savior will immediately enter the devastating seven-year Tribulation, which is the wrath of God poured out in judgment.

Paul points out to the Christians in the 1st Century that they were not in darkness, that the day would overtake them as a thief because they are the children of the light and of the day. Do not misunderstand that Paul was teaching believers in the early church. There is no question the discourse stresses the sudden and imminent return of Christ followed by the catastrophic events of the Tribulation. The passage plainly says believers would not be caught unaware and be a part of the destruction that comes to the world.

God Sends Strong Delusion to Unbelievers Who Reject Christ In the Church Age

There has been much debate as to the meaning of 2 Thessalonians 2:11-12, "And for this cause God shall send them strong delusion, that they should believe a lie: That they all might be damned who believed not the truth, but had pleasure in unrighteousness." (2 Thessalonians 2:11-12) Those whom God sends a strong delusion, to believe a lie, are stated as those who have not believed and had pleasure in unrighteousness. False doctrine, as perpetrated by the false prophet, will abound in the seven years of desolation. God states He sends these unbelievers in the seven years, the strong delusion to believe the lies of a false and world-wide religion. The question is why He takes this action? Because of taking pleasure in unrighteousness before the rapture, these will not receive the love of the truth and thus damn themselves. Evidently this in time would before the Tribulation and continue into the period.

It seems one can correctly conclude that those who heard the Gospel prior to the Tribulation and did not believe the truth and rejected the saving Gospel of Jesus Christ are the ones who are sent the strong delusion. Because of their unbelief and rejection of truth, they will not be saved and not raptured. Apparently, the Holy Spirit does not bring conviction to these unbelievers and God's longsuffering comes to an end. They are allowed to follow the Antichrist's false religion without the intervention of the Holy Spirit's convicting ministry.

Those who receive the strong delusion are probably <u>not</u> those who merely heard about Jesus Christ but never in their hearts made a conscience decision to reject Him. Most of the world has heard of Jesus Christ but know little about Him or about God's truth. Millions will be saved in the seven years who for the first time hear the truth and accept it.

The Last Days

Without question Christians have been in the "last days" since Christ's return to heaven. John explained, "Little children, it is the last time: and as ye have heard that antichrist shall come, even now are there many antichrists; <u>whereby we know that it is the last time</u>." (1 John 2:18) [emphasis added] Therefore being in the last days since the first century means Christians have been looking for the imminent return of Christ since the time of the early churches.

When God revealed the mystery of the rapture, He concluded the revelation with the words *"Wherefore comfort one another with these words."* (1 Thessalonians 4:18) How could there be any comfort in knowing, that as the bride of Christ, the Church Age saints would have to endure part of the horrible events that will come to those on the earth. Matthew describes this seven year as "For then shall be great tribulation, such as was not since the beginning of the world to this time, no, nor ever shall be." (Matthew 24:21)

Further, in 1 Thessalonians 5:9 after warning about the absolute surety of the rapture and the devastation that the unsaved would face being left on earth Paul gave assurance that Christians would not experience the wrath of God. "For God hath not appointed us to wrath, but to obtain salvation by our Lord Jesus Christ, Who died for us, that, whether we wake or sleep, we should live together with him." (1 Thessalonians 5:9-10)

Some have falsely concluded that the "wrath of God" does not immediately begin when the Tribulation starts. They teach the wrath of God refers to the judgments beginning around the time of the seventh Seal Judgment. They explain that the Seal Judgments are the wrath of man or the Satan empowered Antichrist and not God. However, that cannot be the case because beginning in Revelation 6:1 and following, clearly states it is Christ who opens each Seal thus initiating these beginning judgments that are the wrath of God.

In beginning His judgments God allows the Antichrist to be His instrument of His wrath. God has throughout history used pagan nations and individuals to bring judgment on His people. With the Holy Spirit restrained it is clear that God is using the Antichrist to accomplish His will. In the fourth, Seal Revelation 6:8 says that God gives the pale horse rider the power to kill a fourth part of the people on earth. It is God who inaugurates this mass genocide on mankind. This means that 1.76 billion people will be killed during the Seal Judgments.

Revelation 6:9-10 records that as the Fifth Seal is opened John saw the souls of them slain for the word of God. Thus, a part of the 1.76 billion people who are killed are martyrs whom the Antichrist has murdered during the time of the Fourth Seal Judgment. These believers were not spared the wrath of God that allowed the Antichrist to persecute and kill them. Clearly, Paul stated that those of the Church Age are not appointed to wrath. (2 Thess. 2:9-20)

Also, God's hand is seen in that the restraining ministry of the Holy Spirit will be suspended when the Tribulation begins. Note what 2 Thessalonians 2:6-12 reveal:

"And now ye know what withholdeth that he might be revealed in his time. For the mystery of iniquity doth already work: only he who now letteth will let, until he be taken out of the way. And then shall that Wicked be revealed, whom the Lord shall consume with the spirit of his mouth, and shall destroy with the brightness of his coming: Even him, whose coming is after the working of Satan with all power and signs and lying wonders, And with all deceivableness of unrighteousness in them that perish; because they received not the love of the truth, that they might be saved. And for this cause God shall send them strong delusion, that they should believe a lie: That they all might be damned who believed not the truth, but had pleasure in unrighteousness." (2 Thessalonians 2:6-12)

God says the Holy Spirit will be "taken out of the way" of Satan and he will have a free hand to bring the disastrous events on the believing Jews and Gentiles on earth. It does not mean the Holy Spirit will not be active in the seven years. He will be bringing conviction to the hearts of men and many will be saved. Further, He will be involved in God judgments of mankind.

Daniel's 70th Week
The Great Tribulation Begins.
Matthew 24-25

Even though the events that Jesus describes have been happening throughout history, the magnitude of these happenings cannot be compared with those of the Tribulation. The daily news warns of the catastrophic, devastation that volcanos, tsunamis, earthquakes, metros and asteroids, famine, and disease could suddenly bring to the world. The magnitude of the past events cannot be compared to what they will do in the Tribulation. Revelation 6:7-8 predict that one quarter of the earth's population will be killed. God has not been pouring out His wrath in the past two thousand years. What is happening today is only a prelude to the fulfilling of Christ's prophecies, but are the embryonic beginnings which will escalate into the catastrophic desolations of the seven years of the Tribulation.

Daniel 24,
24. "Seventy weeks are determined upon thy people and upon thy holy city, to finish the transgression, and to make an end of sins, and to make reconciliation for iniquity, and to bring in everlasting righteousness, and to seal up the vision and prophecy, and to anoint the most Holy.

25. Know therefore and understand, that from the going forth of the commandment to restore and to build Jerusalem unto the Messiah the Prince shall be seven weeks, and threescore and two weeks: the street shall be built again, and the wall, even in troublous times.
26. And after threescore and two weeks shall Messiah be cut off, but not for himself: and the people of the prince that shall come shall destroy the city and the sanctuary; and the end thereof shall be with a flood, and unto the end of the war desolations are determined.
27. And he shall confirm the covenant with many for one week: and in the midst of the week he shall cause the sacrifice and the oblation to cease, and for the overspreading of abominations he shall make it desolate, even until the consummation, and that determined shall be poured upon the desolate." (Daniel 9:24-27)

Daniel said this last week, as verse 27 reveals, will conclude the Old Testament and will end with the Messiah; (1) ending the transgression and sin of Israel, (2) to make the reconciliation for iniquity, (3) to bring in everlasting righteousness, (4) to seal up the vision and prophecy, and (5) to anoint the most Holy (Second Coming and establishing His kingdom.

Only one of these five goals Daniel predicted has been accomplished. Jesus made the "reconciliation for iniquity" which was His redemptive work on the cross where He with His shed blood paid the sin debt of the world. The other four elements in God's plan have not been accomplished yet. This is strong evidence that the present Church Age is not part of the Old Testament dispensation and is a separate economy of God's overall program for the world. When Israel rejected Jesus as their Messiah, clearly God interjected this present dispensation in which He would gather to Himself a bride from among the Gentiles.

Nothing in God's word even hints that God's purposes for Israel, as expressed by Daniel 9:24, were put aside. They were only moved to a later time which is yet future to this age. Thus, with the beginning of Revelation 6 the Old Testament dispensation ends. This is followed by the outpouring of the Seal Judgments and the last week of Daniel's Seventy weeks will unfold. At the end of this last week the Messiah will purge the Earth and be anointed the Righteous King, who sets up His Kingdom and rules in the Millennium. The Church Age is not in view having ended with the rapture of all the saints of God who have been saved since Pentecost, meaning born again Christians of this current Church Age."[6]

---

[6] Cooper P. Abrams, III, A Commentary of the Book of Revelation, *The Revelation of Jesus Christ,* THE SEAL JUDGMENTS, REVELATION 6:1-17, (http://bible-truth.org/Revelation-Chapter6.doc.) 2013.

The Sequence of These Events

Matthew 24

24:5 - **Many will come and claim to be Christ.**

24:6-7 – **There will be wars and rumors of wars, nation against nation, kingdom against kingdom famines, pestilences, and earthquakes in many places.** Ethnic groups can be included in the word "nation."

24:8 - **These things are the beginning of sorrows (birth pains).**

24:9 – **Believers will be persecuted, martyred and hated by the unbelieving world.**

24:10 – **There will be open apostasy, betrayal, and hatred among those professing to be believers.**

24:11 - **Many false prophets will deceive many.**

24:12 - **Iniquity shall abound, and the love of many will grow cold.**

24:13 - God promises physical salvation to those who would endure and survive to the end. These are saved people who will go into the Millennial kingdom in their natural bodies and repopulate the earth. (This is not a reference to spiritual salvation. Salvation is not received during any age through the works of man. (Eph. 2:8-9) Salvation is received by faith and is a free gift of God.)

24:14 - The "Gospel of the Kingdom" shall be preached unto all nations and then the end comes. This is probably accomplished by the 144,000 sealed Jews. Note the Gospel is specifically stated as being the Gospel of the Kingdom. All men are saved by accepting by faith in the Gospel that has been preached since the early churches. (1 Cor. 15:1-5) However, this statement specifically states it is the Gospel of the Kingdom that is preached. The Gospel of the Kingdom is for Israel and announces their promised Kingdom. This verse is not addressing this Church Age. God is renewing His offer of the Kingdom to Israel. (Jer. 33:10-16)

This preaching of the Gospel in all the nations will occur during the Tribulation, not in our present age. In spite of the great evangelistic work that has and is being done on earth only a fraction of the nations of the earth have a clear Gospel witness. Biblical mission organizations estimate that only about half the country has actually heard a true Gospel witness. Many have heard about Jesus Christ but do not really know who He is or what He did by coming to earth. Many, such as the cults, have been deceived and deny His deity and are worshipping a false Christ. They have not truly heard who Christ is and His plan of salvation. However, in God's mercy and grace, He will cause all on earth to hear the Gospel. (Matt. 24:14) Even as it is today it appears a great many will reject Him, however, as Revelation 6:8-11, 7:1:17 reveal there will be an innumerable number of people saved during the Tribulation.

24:15 - **Temple will be defiled by the Antichrist.** (Dan. 9:27) This is the Tribulation temple and would seem to place the time about the middle of the seven years when Satan is cast to the earth and possesses the Antichrist.

24:16-20 - **Those in Judea flee to the mountains.** How can one relate this to the present Church Age? Geographically and specifically Jesus is referring to Jews in Israel who were asking about His setting up the Kingdom. He explains to the Jews in Judea, Israel to flee to the mountains to avoid what is about to happen.

THE OLIVET DISCOURSE

24:21 - Then shall be the "great tribulation." The magnitude and scope of these events have no parallel in history, past or present. Many believe this is a reference to the bowl or vial judgments of Revelation 15-18 which occur from the middle to the end of the Seven Year Tribulation. The judgment begins with Christ opening each of the Seal Judgments and will continue into the Trumpet and Vial judgments, thus the devastation will grow progressively worse.

24:22 - The devastation on earth will be the worse the world has ever seen and if God did not shorten the days, no one would be left alive. Satan directing the Antichrist will be raging completely out of control in these last days. He will be intent on destroying all life on earth, thus ending God's plans.

24:23-26 – Unbelievers and evil men will use the crisis for personal gain and many will present themselves as messiahs, offering to save or give relief from the suffering. They will be doing great contrived miracles and trickery (signs) to support their deception. Jesus spoke of false miracles in Matthew 7:22-23 done by "workers of iniquity." What foolish and depraved men these will be who even after experiencing God's judgment on the earth will seek to make merchandise of the situation. In desperation, people will be seeking help and will be told of messiahs who are in the desert or who are apparently secluding themselves from the public.

24:27 - **The reference to lightning coming from the east and shining to the west is an illustration of the suddenness of Christ's return.**

24:28 – **In Ezekiel 39:17-19 and Revelation 19:17-18 mentions the birds eating carrion after Armageddon.** God will destroy the nations gathered in the Jezreel Valley who are fighting each other in the Armageddon war.

24:29 - **Immediately after the "tribulation," the sun and moon go dark, and the stars fall from heaven, and the powers of the heavens will be shaken.** Note this is a Universal event not just a shower of meteors or few asteroids hitting the earth. The whole Universe is shaken.

The Second Coming of Christ

24:30 – There will be a visible sign in the heavens of Christ's coming. It is not the rapture because in many areas there are few if any believers. What this sign will be, is not revealed, but everyone on earth will see it and know it means Christ is returning. This is in counter distinction to the teaching of the imminent return of Christ presented in the Epistles to the churches in this present Church Age. Believers in this dispensation are not told to look for signs, but to look for Christ's imminent return. Paul states that signs relate to the Jews, not the Gentiles. *"For the Jews require a sign, and the Greeks seek after wisdom."* (1 Cor. 1:22)

24:31 - Christ sends his angels with a great sound of a trumpet to gather His "elect" from "the four corners of the wind and one end of heaven to the other." This happens at the Second Coming of the Lord Jesus.

Revelation 14:13-16 reveals the second reaping or rapture of believers as an angel of the Lord reaps believers from the earth as the Lord Jesus commands and watches. (Rev. 14:13)

The believers of this present Church Age being the "bride of Christ" will have been raptured before the seven-year Tribulation began. At the Second Coming they will accompany Christ Jesus, along with the saints throughout the ages past as He returns to earth. On the earth, those who have believed that are still alive and remain until the Second Coming will be gathered to Jerusalem to meet the Savior.

<u>This is **not** the rapture of Church Age saints because the details and timing of these two events are different.</u> Here in Matthew 24:31, Christ sends angels to gather the saints to be present at His arrival. In 1 Thessalonians 4:16-17, states that Christ Himself will descend with a shout and the dead in Christ shall rise first and those alive will be changed and "caught up" (raptured) to meet the Lord in the air. No angels are involved. 1 Corinthians 15:51-52, states that those caught up will be changed in the "twinkling of an eye." The "gathering" of the saints by angels clearly is a different event than the instantaneous "catching up" of Christians of this age in the rapture.

24:32-35 – **The Parable of the Fig Tree.** Jesus uses the process by which a fig tree produces fruit as an illustration of relating the sign He has just mentioned in His Second Coming. He is saying that

THE OLIVET DISCOURSE

as you see these events or signs happening look for the Second Coming and the age to end. As stated, earlier Christians in this age are never told to look for signs, but to be always ready.

Jesus is now answering the disciple's question as to when the Kingdom would be set up. Up to this point He is telling them what the signs would be. There is no correlation between 1 Thess. 4:16, and Matthew 24:31. In 1 Thess. 4:16, there is the voice of "one" angel, identified as the archangel. In Matthew 24:31, Christ sends forth, a plurality of angels, meaning more than one. Contextually, the "elect" of Matthew 24:22 are the same "elect" of Matthew 24:31, which are on the earth during the Tribulation.

24:36-39 – **The comparison to the days of Noah.** Only God knows the hour of His coming. "BUT" Jesus says it will be like it was in the time before the Flood. Noah preached for one hundred and twenty years and worked to complete the ark. He too did not know when the Flood would come, but he continued faithful preparing the ark. Jesus is predicting a long interval between His leaving and His promised return. Using Noah as an example of perseverance and faith He is telling them not to give up hope during the long interval.

The Rapture of the Lost

24:40-41 – **This describes the rapture of the lost.** This is not, the Rapture of the Christians in this the Church Age. The context places this event at the Second Coming which ends the Tribulation. The ones that are taken are taken in judgment and parallel those taken in judgment in the Flood. In the Flood those that were taken were lost and those left were saved. At the Second Coming Christ will remove the unsaved from the earth in judgment. (See Ezek. 20:38, Mt. 8:12, 13:41-42,49-50, 25:41, 2 Thess. 1:7-9). The saints alive at the Second Coming will remain and enter the Kingdom in their natural bodies (Isa. 4:3, Ezek. 20:40-42, Zech. 13:8-9, Matt. 13:43, 24:34). Those alive on the earth at the Second Coming will include the Gentiles and the Jews who believed during the seven years and are the remnant God promised would remain alive and be saved. (See Isa. 10:21-22, 11:11)

<u>This cannot be the Rapture, because you would have all the saints removed from the earth, thus no one to populate the Millennial Kingdom in their **natural unglorified** bodies.</u> Further, at the beginning of the Millennial Kingdom there would only be the lost left on earth. This clearly cannot be

THE OLIVET DISCOURSE

referring to the rapture of believers of this present Church Age, as the whole of the Olivet Discourse is dealing with the 70th Week of Daniel and relates to Israel.

24:42-44 – The Parable of the Householder. This is a warning to the Jews in the Tribulation to watch and be ready for Christ's arrival at the Second Coming.

24:45-51 – The Parable of the Wise Servant. Note that in each parable there is a warning to watch for the signs and get ready. Jesus said in 24:32-34 to watch for the signs and used the illustration of the changing of the seasons. Again, it needs to be stated that believers in the church age, who are the Bride and Body of Christ, are told to look for His imminent return. We today are not told to look for signs, but to be ready to be caught up at any second to meet the Lord. *"For the Jews require a sign, and the Greeks seek after wisdom."* (1 Corinthians 1:22)

The Marriage Supper of The Lamb

Matthew 25

25:1-13 - **Parable of the Ten Virgins.** Again, Jesus is using a parable to warn the nation of Israel, and those living in the Tribulation, to be ready for His coming as their Messiah and the subsequent promised Kingdom. This verse specifically states that the coming Kingdom is "likened" to ten virgins. These are Jewish virgins as only the Jews will be looking for the bridegroom.

The virgins of this parable are invited guests to the wedding of the Bride Groom. The picture is the wedding of the Bride Groom who clearly is the Lord Jesus Christ. Only those saved in this dispensation, the Church Age, are called the bride of Christ. (Matt. 21:9) The virgins clearly are not the bride, but guests to the wedding. The guests, who are living in the Tribulation, are who are told to be ready for the Bridegrooms arrival. Christ's invitation to believe and be saved is to all men on earth. Yet, only those who have believed in this age will be saved and attend the Marriage Supper of the Lamb.

Clearly, it is a serious mistake to conclude that those who are looking for the coming of the

THE OLIVET DISCOURSE

Bride Groom are Church Age believers. They are the bride and they are already prepared. They have been resurrected at the rapture before the seven years begin and judged at the BEMA judgment of Christians. They in their new bodies and pure prepared for the wedding day. The bride is waiting for her bridegroom the Lamb, and the marriage supper.

However, here the invited guests, who are the Jews, in the seven-year Tribulation, are being warned to be ready for Christ's Second Coming. The point is this: Jesus is challenging all the Jews and those alive during the Tribulation to look for the signs He mentioned earlier. They will see the signs of the times, and realized the Messiah will soon come and make themselves ready for Him. The description of the seal, trumpet, and bowl judgments constitute the signs that will be apparent. Both the wise and the foolish virgins were aware that the Bridegroom would soon arrive.

Those who reject Christ's message and the signs in this parable are referred to as foolish virgins who were not prepared. They will miss the Bridegroom and His wedding. In other words, the wise virgins were ready and entered into the Millennial Kingdom, and the foolish virgins not being prepared and were rejected. It is vital to understand that the judgments in the Tribulation are poured on the earth to warn men of Christ's return. The Old Testament abounds the forewarnings of the Messiah's coming. God is longsuffering and desires all to be saved. Each time in God's word where God is bringing judgment, He also is offering salvation if they repent and believe.

Revelation 19:7-9 is the first reference to believers of the Church Age since Revelation 2-3. This is describing the Marriage Supper of the Lamb. Those invited to the Marriage Supper are guests and the guests are those living after Christ's bride is raptured. Verse 19, specifically distinguishes between the bride and the invited guests to the wedding. "And he saith unto me, Write, Blessed are they which are called unto the marriage supper of the Lamb. And he saith unto me, These are the true sayings of God." (Revelation 19:9) The invited guests will be the Jews and Gentiles saved during the seven years of Tribulation.

25:14-30 – **The Parable of the Talents**. Once again, Jesus is using the term "For the kingdom of heaven are "liken to" or "as". This sets the context of His remarks. Jesus in this parable presents a contrast between those who looked for the Master's return and wisely used their talents and those who did not. They all knew the Master would return and require an accounting of them. Two servants faithfully used what they were given, but the third was slothful and indifferent and he was condemned. The unprofitable servant was cast into outer darkness which is a reference to hell. In the context of the parable, Jesus is saying to Israel that they should be looking for the Master's return and use the talents they have been given. Verse 29 makes the point that Israel had the knowledge of the Messiah and the coming Kingdom. They had been given much and therefore they would be judged accordingly. They had the privilege of the Old Testament scriptures, the prophecies of the coming Messiah, seeing Him, hearing his preaching, and seeing His miracles. For the most part, the majority of Israel rejected all this truth they had been given.

The Second Coming of Christ
The Judgment of the Nations

25:31 - Jesus then says the Kingdom would begin when He comes with all His angels and sets on the throne. Those on earth, whom God purges at His coming, will be cast into Gehenna, where there will be weeping and gnashing of teeth. Matthew 8:11-12 reveals many Jews will not be among those who enter the Kingdom, but many Gentiles will. "And I say unto you, That many shall come from the east and west, and shall sit down with Abraham, and Isaac, and Jacob, in the kingdom of heaven. But the children of the kingdom shall be cast out into outer darkness: there shall be weeping and gnashing of teeth." (Matthew 8:11-12)

What a tragedy this is, as those who had been given the truth, could have believed. But realize they have no further chance and are condemned in the torment of "outer darkness." The gnashing of teeth pictures the intense pain and regret they are experiencing.

The Judgment of Nations

25:32--33 The Judgment of the people of all nations is referred to as the sheep and goat judgment. This is a judgment of the individual Gentiles nations who are alive at the Second Coming having survived the seven-year Tribulation. This is referred to the "Judgment of Nations" as verse 32 states all nations will be gathered before Him. However, the use of the word "nations" refers to individuals of these nations, not a whole nation or a nation as a whole. No nation is made up of all saved or all unsaved people, thus the judgment is of individuals of the nations of earth. This judgment is referred to in Joel 3:1-3:

"For, behold, in those days, and in that time, when I shall bring again the captivity of Judah and Jerusalem, I will also gather all nations, and will bring them down into the valley of Jehoshaphat, and will plead with them there for my people and for my heritage Israel, whom they have scattered among the nations, and parted my land. And they have cast lots for my people; and have given a boy for an harlot, and sold a girl for wine, that they might drink." (Joel 3:1-3)

This judgment will be one of separation or division of the "sheep, meaning believers, on His right and on His left the "goats" who are unbelievers. It will occur after the Second Coming and before the Lord sets up the Millennial kingdom. Some have mistakenly thought this is a final judgment of mankind with the sheep being saved and the goats being lost. It is not. This judgment is for those who lived through the seven years. Those saved will enter the Millennium and the lost into Hades to await the final judgment. (Matt. 25:46) The final judgment of the unsaved is recorded in Revelation 20:11-15 and includes all men who have died on earth. (Rev. 20:12, 14) Verse 14 states this is the second death. Thus, all men who rejected the Lord will be judged according to their sins and cast into the Lake of Fire.

25:34 Note that this judgment of the Gentiles takes place when Jesus returns, after the Second Coming. This judgment occurs on earth at the Second Coming as the Lord divides the saved from the lost living inhabitants of this world. All at the this judgment come in their natural bodies. The lost are those on earth who are purged from the earth. The saved, are those on earth who believed and by faith were forgiven, saved and physically survived the seven-year Tribulation and will go into the Millennium in their physical bodies.

THE OLIVET DISCOURSE

It is important to recognize that there is no resurrection involved here and no mention of a judgment of the dead. (See Rev. 20:11-15 for the judgment of unbelievers) God is judging all people who have survived the seven-year Tribulation, both saved and lost. Joel 3:2 says it will take place in the Valley of Jehoshaphat. Some believe this is the Valley of Berachah (2 Chron. 20:26) where Jehoshaphat defeated the Moabites and Ammorties, which gave the valley a new name. Others refer to the place as being the Valley of Kidron outside Jerusalem. Some refer to Zechariah 14:4, which says the Lord will return to the Mount of Olives and a great valley will be opened. Jehoshaphat means "Jehovah judges." It seems probable that this takes place in the Valley of Jehoshaphat as the name of this new valley implies a judgment. Here Christ will judge the nations. No one can be dogmatic as to the place of this judgment because the place is not revealed, however, your writer holds to the latter view, which seems to be more likely.

25:35-46 - **The basis of this judgment is based on how they treated "my brethren" (Matt. 25:40)**. This refers how these how saved Gentiles treated the saved Jews that they had contact with during the Tribulation. What is interesting is that these saved Gentiles, in their benevolence to the Jews, did not seem to be aware of the importance to Christ of His brethren. No one should ever miss the fact that the Jews are God's chosen people. Clearly, the Lord has a special place in His heart for, those of His chosen nation who accept Him as their Messiah. Paul confirms this in Romans 9:6, "Not as though the word of God hath taken none effect. For they are not all Israel, which are of Israel." These saved Gentiles simply did what was right in helping their fellow believers who happened to be Jews. It is well to understand the Antichrist will unleash his most terrible persecution against the Jews.

God sends, at the beginning of the Tribulation, 144,000 Jewish evangelists who preach all over the world. (Rev. 7:1-8, 14:1-5) It should be noted that today, in this dispensation, the responsibility in the 1st Century to spread the Gospel was given to His disciples the command to teach all nations the Gospel. (Matthew 28:19-20). Subsequently the commission is given to all Christians since. However, with all Christians removed from the earth at the rapture, God calls and seals the 144,000 Jews to be His witness in the seven Tribulation years. This is further evidence of the Pre-Tribulational rapture. It will be these Jews who appropriately will be sent to evangelize their

THE OLIVET DISCOURSE

fellow Jews and also to the Gentiles. They will be the one's preaching the Gospel of the Kingdom to every nation.

This judgment of nations is based on how the Gentiles receive these Jewish preachers, and the Jews who believe in Christ during this period. This is further evidence that the seven-year Tribulation is a Jewish event. These Gentiles also believe the Gospel and are saved. The persecution of Jews will be greater that Gentiles. These saved Gentiles aided the Jews who were being persecuted by the Antichrist. Jesus calls them "blessed" and tells them that the Kingdom was also prepared for them before the foundation of the world.

Some "biblical" scholars and churches today state that God is finished with the Jews. In their "replacement" theology they claim God has replaced Israel with "the church". First, there is not such institution of "the" church with is an erroneous statement that concludes there is a universal "church". The word translated church in the New Testament refers exclusively to an "ekklesia" or assembly of believers. There is not a universal institution in the Church Age, but many believers assembling themselves to worship and serve the Lord Jesus. Jesus' own words completely disprove their false assumption of any "replacement theology".

"For Israel *hath* not *been* forsaken, nor Judah of his God, of the LORD of hosts; though their land was filled with sin against the Holy One of Israel." (Jeremiah 51:5)

"And so all Israel shall be saved: as it is written, There shall come out of Sion the Deliverer, and shall turn away ungodliness from Jacob: For this *is* my covenant unto them, when I shall take away their sins." (Romans 11:26-27)

"*But* Israel shall be saved in the LORD with an everlasting salvation: ye shall not be ashamed nor confounded world without end." (Isaiah 45:17)

God's promise and covenant with Abraham and his descendants was an "everlasting" covenant. "And I will establish my covenant between me and thee and thy seed after thee in their generations for an everlasting covenant, to be a God unto thee, and to thy seed after thee." (Genesis 17:7)

The main focus of the Antichrist, who is possessed by Satan, will be to destroy the Jews in the Tribulation. Even at this time, when he sees the

THE OLIVET DISCOURSE

Lord pouring out judgment on those who reject Him, Satan will continue to hinder and try to destroy the Lord's plans. If the Jews could be destroyed, the Millennial and the promised Kingdom of Israel would not occur, thus God would default on His promises. Thus, Satan's goal is to use the Antichrist and his forces to destroy the Jews from off the earth.

This is not a judgment that imparts salvation to those who have worked for their salvation by doing the good deeds of helping these Jews. Salvation is never received because of one's good works. (Eph. 2:8-9, Rom. 4:5) The works of compassion shown to the saved Jews is evidence that these Gentiles, who are to be part of the Kingdom, and believed the message that Jesus was the Messiah (Savior) and accepted Him as their Savior. The Gentiles will also have the witness of the 144,000, and the scriptures that plainly reveal the judgments they are seeing are from God. Those who by faith accepted God's word are saved in the same way all men are saved, by believing and receiving Jesus Christ (Messiah) as their Savior.

The result for these, who believed, both Jew and Gentile, is that they enter into the Kingdom alive in their natural bodies. They are not

THE OLIVET DISCOURSE

resurrected, but remain in their human bodies unchanged. They then repopulate the world during the 1000-year reign of Jesus Christ on earth. This explains who will be the earthly inhabitants of the Millennial Kingdom. This fulfills the prophecies of Daniel 7:14, Isa. 55:4-6, and Micah 4:1-2 which states a large group of Gentiles will have a part in the kingdom. Although most of the Jews never accepted Him in the Old Testament, God plainly revealed that the Gentiles would accept Him and be a part of the Kingdom promised to Israel. (See Psa. 2:1-10; Isa. 63:1-6; Joel 3:2-16; Zeph. 3:8; Zech. 14:1-3)

Note also that there will be many saved Jews alive and these will be the ones who actually inherit the earth in the Millennium kingdom. Saved the Jews who have died will be resurrected and in their spiritual bodies they too will take part in the kingdom in the same way as Christians who are saved in the current age.

The "goats" are pictured on the left hand of the Savior, as Matthew 25:41 states and they are condemned and their final destiny consigned, *"into everlasting fire prepared for the devil and his angels."* The judgment they are consigned to is Gehenna that follows the Great White Throne Judgment of Revelation 20:11-15.

THE OLIVET DISCOURSE

They had the same opportunity as the "sheep" that received the Gospel and repented of their sins. They heard the message of the 144,000 and other saints saved during this period, but rejected it and thus sealed their eternal doom.

Matthew 24:40-41 explains that those who reject the Messiah during the Tribulation will be caught up, removed from the earth and judged. Those left on earth are saved people, the elect, who will enter the Kingdom Age.

Matthew 24:14 describes the place of their judgment is the, "everlasting fire prepared for the devil and his angels." This plainly is a reference to "Gehenna" the "Lake of Fire" (Revelations 20:14) and not to "Hades" the present abode of the unsaved dead. Satan is never said to be in Hades, the present abode of the lost who are awaiting the final judgment or his angels. Revelations 20:10, says that Satan will be thrown into the Lake of Fire, before the judgments of the unsaved lost at the Great White Throne judgment (Revelations 20:11-15). Thus, this verse is saying the unsaved of the Great Tribulation are judged and condemned immediately and cast into the eternal Lake of Fire and are not a part of the Great White Throne judgment that happens after the Millennium.

Conclusion

As Warren Wiersbe said, "Next to the 13th chapter, no part of Matthew has suffered more misinterpretation than the chapters 24-25! Almost every major cult has used Matthew 14:1-41, along with Daniel 9:20-27, to "prove" that Christ has already returned! Even well-meaning yet unlearned evangelicals confuse the issue by applying this section to the church in this age."[7]

Every detail of Matthew 24-25 is related to the Jews and the nation of Israel. In the Old Testament God's focus was in Israel, but the Gentiles were also saved through their relationship with the Lord's chosen people. It will be the same in the seven-year Tribulation.

There is nothing in these two chapters which relates to the present church age or believers of this dispensation. It is therefore a serious mistaken to interpret the Olivet Discourse as referring to end of the Church Age and there is no support for a Pre-wrath, Mid, or Post Tribulational rapture, or Amillennialism. If understood properly, these passages support the doctrine of a Pre-

---

[7] Warren W. Wiersbe, Expository Outlines on the New Testament, Calvary Book Room, Covington, KY, 1982, p61

THE OLIVET DISCOURSE

Tribulational rapture of believers in this present Church Age and of the Pre-Millennial return of the Lord Jesus Christ.

Matthew 24-25 addresses the events of the Tribulation, which is the final seven years of Daniel's 490 year prophecy that ends with the Messiah coming to reign in power. Christ's Second Coming will end the Old Testament dispensation and not the Church Age which ends earlier at the rapture.

Jesus' ministry was in the Old Testament dispensation. So far only 483 years of Daniel's prophecy has transpired which leaves the final seven years (Daniel's 70th Week) still future. The Old Testament dispensation is not completed, but will be finished with the coming of the Messiah at the end of the last week. Thus, none of the statements in Matthew 24-25 refer to the Church Age or Church Age saints.

To labor the point, clearly Christians are not present or mentioned in the Tribulation events of Matthew 24-25, nor in Revelation 4-19. Yes, an innumerable amount of people will be saved during the Tribulation which will include Jews and Gentiles (Matt. 24:14). This begins at the opening of the Tribulation period with God saving and sealing

144,000 Jews. If Christians in the Church Age are present during the Tribulation, why did He not include Gentiles as well in calling and sealing this special group of believers? The absence of Gentiles plainly shows the Jewish nature and focus and the emphasis of Daniel's 70th Week that ends the Old Testament dispensation. These saved people will be Old Testament saints, not Christians and not the body of or Bride of Christ. The Tribulation is a Jewish event when God will restore Israel, the Temple worship, and save a remnant of the Jews and Gentiles who will populate the earth in the Millennium and fulfill His unconditional promises and covenant with His chosen people, the nation of Israel.

The modern teachers of the Pre-Wrath, Middle and Post Tribulational views are making the same mistake the Judaizers that Paul dealt with in the early churches. They mix God's promises to the nation of Israel with that of Christians in the Church Age. Clearly, God through Paul condemned this false interpretation of His word.

Mixing God's promises to Israel with those of Christians in this the Church Age is also the error of the cults, Pentecostals, Charismatics, Amillennialists, the Reformed movement replacement theology, and those who purport the

Lord will cause His bride to go through the catastrophic events of the Tribulation. These false teachers fail to understand the context and emphasis of the Gospels and God's separate programs for Israel. They have no "comfort" that God offers in 1 Thess. 4:18. The Gentile has a common Gospel (1 Cor. 15:1-5, note Matt. 4:17) and are grafted into the God's plan for Israel. Christians in this age are not Israel and God has a different destiny for us. He also has not abandoned His plans and promises to Israel as a nation which is the main focus of the coming seven-year Tribulation. Further, God has promised the blessed hope which is to come for the believers in this the Church Age, in the rapture that precedes the Tribulation.

"He which testifieth these things saith, Surely I come quickly. Amen. Even so, come, Lord Jesus." (Revelation 22:20)

ABOUT THE AUTHOR

Pastor Cooper Abrams is a veteran missionary, pastor, church planter, and author working in the state of Utah since 1986. He and his wife Carolyn are missionaries sent by Calvary Baptist Church, King, NC and have been involved in seeing three sound Independent Baptist churches established in Utah since 1986 and numerous other churches helped in the Inter-mountain West.

He graduated from Piedmont Baptist College in 1981 with a Th.B. (Bachelor of Theology), and in 2000 with an MBS (Master of Biblical Studies). In 2013, he earned a Ph.D. in Biblical Studies from Bethany Divinity College and Seminary.

He is an avid writer and has authored numerous articles, books, Bible courses, and six Bible commentaries. He has written many articles on apologetics, hermeneutics, Baptist History, The Pentecostal Movement, and Mormonism.

Most of his work is posted on his popular Internet website, Bible Truth **http://bible-truth.org**. The

THE OLIVET DISCOURSE

website which was begun in 1996 currently averages over five hundred visitors per day. The site is rated among the top two to five Baptist websites, out of thousands of Baptist web sites. There are hundreds of KJV sermons, articles on various biblical subjects, and information on Mormonism can be found on the web site.

He can be contacted at: cpabrams3@gmail.com

www.ingramcontent.com/pod-product-compliance
Lightning Source LLC
Chambersburg PA
CBHW071719040426
42446CB00011B/2139